When The Willow Weeps

Tyana Kline

Presentation by *BookLeaf Publishing*

Web: www.bookleafpub.com

E-mail: info@bookleafpub.com

ISBN: 9789357212465

First edition 2023

ACKNOWLEDGEMENT

Thankful to my family for talking me into my hobby of writing again.

To my amazing daughters, you feed my strength and restore my peace. My son you always somehow manage to lift me up, and at the same time hold me down. For your encouragement, I am thankful. My beautiful grandchildren, you are the keepers of my heart.

And to my husband, thank you for withstanding the storms, always hand in mine, and giving me the space to heal.

You have each supported and encouraged me through this journey. You have fed my spirit and I am ever grateful.

To my beautiful grandmother, may she forever rest in loving energy. Resonating with her strength and wisdom has always been my saving grace.

PREFACE

Surviving our most fearful times brings about our greatest growth.

This collection of short poems can sad, and heart-tugging, but the healing process requires a deep look and compassionate forgiveness.

I felt my way through writing these poems during some of the darkest times of my healing journey.

Through past painful situations, I hope to empower those of you who are on your journey and inspire you to explore the level of healing that comes with facing yourself in the dark.

Set Me Free

Whence burdened and worn from owing life's
fee
My first request and my final plea
Give me the sun the sand, and the sea
Lest I be bound to never be free

Daddy's Boy

don't give up daddy
please fight for me
this is my prayer
before going to sleep

mommy took me away but
she cannot be
all that I need daddy
why won't she see

i'm a big boy now but
it's hard for me
understanding all this because
i'm only 3

i cried lots of tears until
i couldn't see
but i knew deep inside
you still wanted me

i miss your hugs
the strength in your voice
i did not want to go, daddy
i had no choice

Play Time

i try to be good
but sometimes it's hard
i wish i could play in the neighbor's backyard

far from their sight
and with all of my might
i wish i could go out and stay

wiped my face clean
so they won't be mean
why do they hate me this way

i'll pretend i'm not sad
so they won't be mad
and wish, for my cries are not heard

the night's almost here
uncovering fear
stay quiet now, don't speak a word

why do they hurt me
leave me so scarred
if i could just play in the neighbor's backyard

At Night I Cry

at night i cry 'til i fall asleep
i must try to keep quiet
and not make a peep

it hurts so much, to know you're not loved
why does this happen
i just wanna be hugged

i've tried to speak up, tho I'm just a child
but she tells them all lies
and her stories are wild

day after day, i pray to leave here
but no one can help
i'm alone with my fear

at night i cry, but i try to be strong
someone, please save me
i can't last too long

Creeper

it's quiet time when mommy's sleeping
the lights are out, the dark is creeping
hanging by my bedroom peeping
innocence he's hungry seeking

close my eyes pretend i'm sleeping
nothing stops this reaper's reaping
please help me, the pain's increasing
"keep it down she'll hear you weeping"

he's done now
i lie here bleeding
he took everything he's needing

quiet now
but inside screaming
completely numb
and barely breathing

My Hero

Superman, you ain't so tough
at least not like me

That big fat S, stuck to your chest
hidden where no one can see

Superman, you haven't shown up
you won't even pick up the phone

You never come, when i'm on the run
you cowardly leave me alone

Superman, where are you, bro
you've been ignoring my cries

If you don't come quick, i'll keep getting hit
it's safer to lay there and die

Superman, dude never mind anymore
don't even know why i had hope

It's just that I'm scared of that fiery red hair
and i'm at the end of her rope

Superman, please when is my turn
i don't think i'll make it to ten

A few more bad things, then i'll have my wings
will you please fly with me then

She Was

Ripped raw
Scared silent
Shut down and froze cold

Gone numb
Left worthless
Mind aching to fold

The hurt inside
The pain
She cries
Wandering into this void

Empty and dead
Whispers
Filling her head
The innocent child now destroyed

Our Wish

Where are you oh little star
It's such a clear crisp night
Thought we'd hang out here with you
But you're nowhere in sight

It's just me and my brother here
Are you available tonight?

We've always wondered what you are
And would like a wish or two
Oh bright diamond in the sky
Please make our life brand new

We'll wish for only happy things
Somewhere in time and space

A safer home
And food to eat
Would be our saving grace

If you could find the time for us
We'd ever be in debt
It's lonely in this awful place
Please help us to forget

Picked

Picked for her beauty
a delicate prize

like dew on a flower
tears swell her eyes

he will
go on
without her
as she's left to die

uprooted
un-grounded
a love full of lies

and yet
picked for her beauty
a delicate prize.

Out Of Balance

Like fire & ice in the same sterling bowl
Rampant with heat, but still running cold

Beautiful eyes that yet, cannot see
Secrets and whispers of what is to be

Hurricane winds on a calm ocean shore
Waves of destruction sent from the core

Emptied of life, nothing to give
No remorse, no recourse, no way to live

Slipping Away

I'm suicidal but not how you think
I've never taken my share

Disturbed and empty, memories gone in a blink
Not sure if anyone's there

It's been a slow death with me on the brink
Constantly changing my hair

Desperate for help but I'll smile and wink
Completely lost in despair

Fog taking over with every drop of this ink
A mind in need of repair

I'm suicidal but not how you think
Don't even know if I care

Confusion

Life in an instant becomes strangled by
confusion
eroding the sweetest love
quickly
and without warning

At a time when life seems grand
it strikes
leaving one blind

Blindsided by this confusion that has risen
like a blazing summer sun

It consumes all happiness
and tears away at your soul

Like a scavenger on the dead
confusion in love is the worst of all
it is a sickness a fatal disease

It will leave you desolate and broken
dangling over the edge
with nothing left
but the fall

Your Scars

I saw your scars today
and it really made me sad
faithful to a brutal love,
that burnt thru all you had

A partner condescending to
the woman at his side
words battering your worth
fists ripping thru your pride

A "Worthless…Stupid...Whore"
despite the good you'd do
toxic to the very core
he had no place with you

I saw your scars today
and I admire them somehow
you hide them oh so gently
but I see more clearly now

Sated by controlling you
a heart as cold as ice
a child instead of man it seems
still tripping through his life

Sit back and let me show you
how empowered women walk
unimpressed by his existence
or the foul bs he talks

I saw your scars today
as reflections not of you
just his feeble mind right there
inside, consuming you

Vacancy

Internal abandonment
No contrast from which to grow

Barren thoughts unspoken
A lifeless uninhabited soul

Devoilé

I would have shown compassion
When I sought to understand
Yet you choose to disrespect me
The mother of our clan

Sneaking in the shadows
So those close to you don't see
I only press against it
Because it shouldn't be

But you care not for family
When you don you mask
Tried to come between us
and could not complete the task

Meticulous deceiver
It seems par for your course
But you forget one thing
My relationship with Source

I've bled and I've let go
Just know that on its way
Is a dish for you or maybe two
Of karma out to play

Their Presence

Awakened from the nightmares
While morning's still dark
They press deep inside me
Their claws within my heart

I feel them all around me
I swear to you I do
Got me trippin on myself
While I'm over here watching you

I see them but I don't want to
I never even try
I see them in the shadows
Just a flicker in the eye

I feel them
Here beside me
They never let me rest
I see them with my eyes closed
Even when I'm at my best

All Alone

when i'm all alone
and the dark inside grows deep
i fall into a slumber
wherein there is no sleep
where demons awaken bright with life
and it's my soul they seek

they move very quickly
like playing peek-a-boo
no one else can see them
and I don't know what to do

they creep from every corner
peering straight at me
only when i try to look
somehow, i just can't see

sometimes i hear them calling
and i don't wanna go
they hide themselves from others
my private horror show

no matter how i medicate
they never leave my side
waiting there inside the void
to take me on a ride

At Home in the Darkness

I am not afraid of darkness. I no longer find fear
in shadows.
Ghosts in the dead of night have become my
friends.

I am not surprised by misfortune. I no longer
look for the "good".
Frustration is most certainly the expectation.

I am not hurt by broken promises. I no longer
trust one's word.
Faith is now the anticipation of deception.

I am not abandoned in loneliness. I no longer
seek hands to hold.
Emptiness became fulfillment leaving me full.

I am not blinded by terror. I no longer see a
light.
Affliction is the affection, my consolation prize.

When you're at peace in this world, there is no
place like "home".

Questions For Nan

Have you ever hurt before, like they used your
heart in vain?

"Darling, I've known the hurt you feel
it always has an end.
But you'll have to pick the pieces up
and build you back again."

Have you ever cried before, when pain ruins
every day?

"I've cried a million tears, my love
they come but they don't stay,
and all the stress built up inside
gets cleanly washed away."

Did you ever feel alone at times, like no one's
there for you?

"Oh, I've felt that lonely cold
but this is what you do.
You take some time and look inside
to warm you thru that too."

Can I come back with questions, just like I did
before?

"Darling, come over and over again,
no one here is keeping score.
I'll always lend a tender hand,
I love you from my core.

Just go sit out there by the sea
and when you pray, you think of me
whenever you need more."

The Shadows Run Deep

before you knew me
you'd swear, i was happy
but now that you're here you can see

before you knew me
you'd swear, i was happy
but now that you're here you can see

i glide like the bird
in those stories you've heard
tho nowhere exists where i'm feeling so free

monsters so real
they know how i feel
always lying there, inside of me

connections destroyed
and i just avoid
love unconditionally

even with friends
i've come to my end
completely lost all of my spark

only scared of myself
never anyone else
longing for walks in the dark

can't pick up the phone
not safe when alone
this is no stroll thru the park

like mental disease
flowing thru us with ease
mother, you have left your mark

Selfless

One day I sat beside myself
along the deep blue sea.

My nanna said she'd meet me here
If I ever felt the need

Well, I had put the world before my self
and was searching for
life's key.

It was my very biggest flaw
I gave the best
of me.

But it took me to a lonely place
and ripped my soul
you see.

Until that day I broke apart
and cried out
endlessly.

I grabbed my pen and wrote a line
tears flowed,
I couldn't see.

I wrote down all the pain inside
the things
I'd dreamed to be.

It took me then quite by surprise
when unbelievably.

My verse gave ways to feel alive
a little taste
of free.

With pen in hand, I purged myself
on the sand
beside the sea.